DANGEROUS DINOS

Sarah Creese

make
believe
ideas

Incredible dinosaurs lived on Earth
millions of years ago.
They were big, small, fierce, and fast—
or sometimes very slow!

Reading together

This book is an ideal first reader for your child, combining simple words and sentences with stunning color images of dinosaurs. Here are some of the many ways you can help your child take those first steps in reading. Encourage your child to:

- Look at and explore the detail in the pictures.
- Sound out the letters in each word.
- Read and repeat each short sentence.

Look at the pictures

Make the most of each page by talking about the pictures and finding key words. Here are some questions you can use to discuss each page as you go along:

- Why do you like this dinosaur?
- What is special about it?
- How big is it?
- What does it eat?

Look at rhymes

Some of the sentences in this book are simple rhymes. Encourage your child to recognize rhyming words. Try asking the following questions:

- What does this word say?
- Can you find a word that rhymes with it?

- Look at the ending of two words that rhyme. Are they spelled the same? For example, "beak" and "weak," and "feet" and "meat."

Test understanding

It is one thing to understand the meaning of individual words, but you need to make sure that your child understands the facts in the text.

- Play "find the obvious mistake." Read the text as your child looks at the words with you, but make an obvious mistake to see if he or she catches it. Ask your child to correct you and provide the right word.
- After reading the facts, close the book and think up questions to ask your child.
- Ask your child whether a fact is true or false.
- Provide your child with three answers to a question and ask him or her to pick the correct one.

Quiz pages

At the end of the book there is a simple quiz. Ask the questions and see if your child can remember the right answers from the text. If not, encourage him or her to look up the answers.

Dinosaurs

Dinosaurs were land animals with sharp horns and teeth, scary claws, and spikes. Some were fierce meat eaters, while others preferred plants.

I'm Tyrannosaurus rex.
I crush and I bite.
I'm strong and I'm fierce,
and I'll give you a fright!

sharp teeth

short arm

tail

I take giant steps
with two large feet.
My favorite meal is
meat, meat, and meat!

(tie-RAN-owe-SORE-uss-REX)
• lived around 67—65
  million years ago
• 13 feet (4 meters) tall

Did you know?

Tyrannosaurus rex was taller than a double-decker bus but had short arms that could not even touch its nose!

I have a long crest
on top of my head.
I don't eat meat;
I eat plants instead.

tail

(par-a-SORE-owe-LOAF-uss)
• lived around 76—74
  million years ago
• 16 feet (4.9 meters) tall

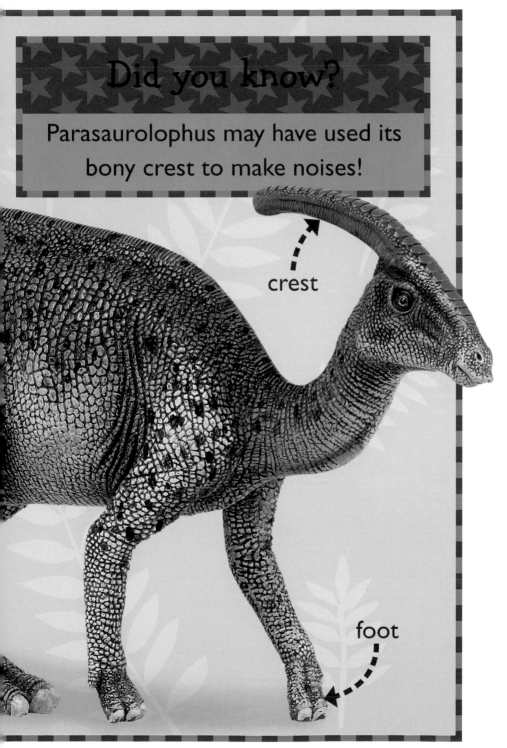

Parasaurolophus may have used its bony crest to make noises!

crest

foot

My large body
is as big as a bus!
Can you guess my name?
It is Steg-o-saur-us!

head

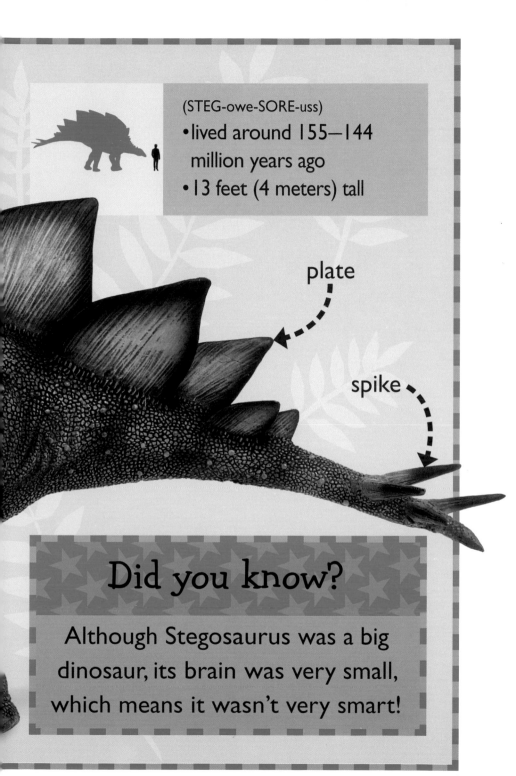

(STEG-owe-SORE-uss)
- lived around 155—144 million years ago
- 13 feet (4 meters) tall

plate

spike

Did you know?

Although Stegosaurus was a big dinosaur, its brain was very small, which means it wasn't very smart!

I have pointy plates
along my back.
They help me keep safe
when enemies attack.

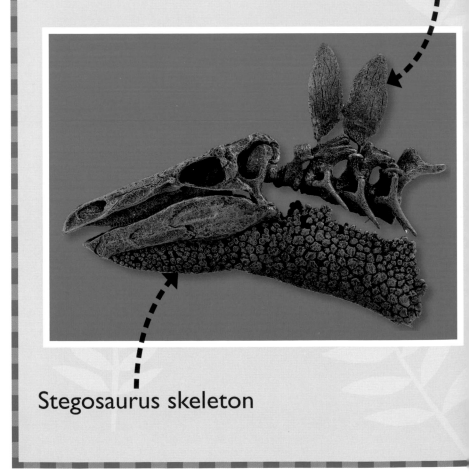

plates

Stegosaurus skeleton

16

Grrrr!

I'm tough and spiky,
and there is no doubt

that I'll use my club-tail
when T rex is about!

Beware!

Did you know?

Ankylosaurus was covered
in armor. It even had
bony eyelids!

(An-KIE-loh-SORE-uss)
- lived around 70—65
  million years ago
- 4 feet (1.2 meters) tall

On my head,
what can you see?
I have three sharp horns—
can you count them with me?

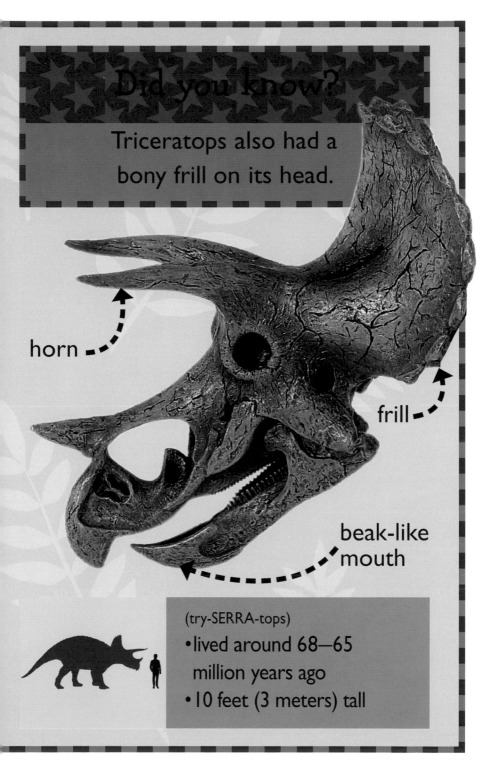

Did you know?

Triceratops also had a bony frill on its head.

horn

frill

beak-like mouth

(try-SERRA-tops)
• lived around 68—65 million years ago
• 10 feet (3 meters) tall

I have lots of teeth.
My mouth looks
like a beak!

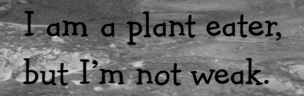

I am a plant eater,
but I'm not weak.

Stretch!

(BRACH-ee-owe-SORE-uss)
- lived around 155—140 million years ago
- 42 feet (13 meters) tall

I'm Brachiosaurus.
I'm a giant dinosaur.
With a long neck and tail,
I am hard to ignore!

Did you know?

Brachiosaurus was about as tall as three double-decker buses!

Velociraptor

I'm fast and smart,
with a strong, thin jaw.
I grab my food using
big, sharp claws!

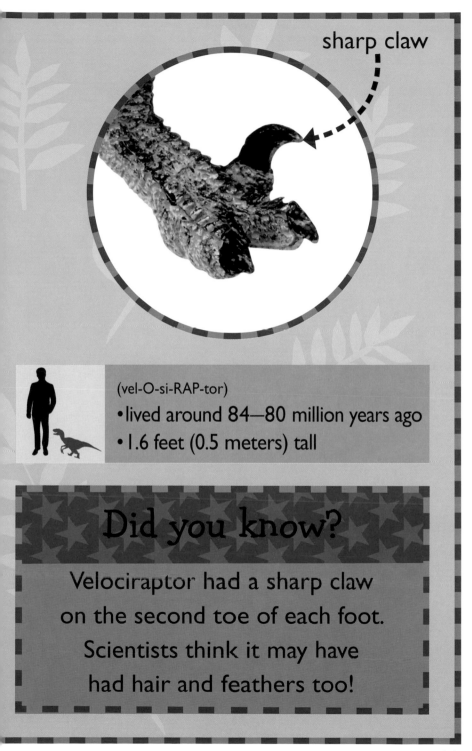

sharp claw

(vel-O-si-RAP-tor)
• lived around 84—80 million years ago
• 1.6 feet (0.5 meters) tall

Did you know?

Velociraptor had a sharp claw
on the second toe of each foot.
Scientists think it may have
had hair and feathers too!

What do you know?

1. Which dinosaur had pointy plates along its back?

2. How tall was Brachiosaurus?

3. Did T rex have short arms or short legs?

4. Which dinosaur had a long crest on top of its head?

5. What did Velociraptor have on each of its second toes?

6. Did Stegosaurus have a large brain or a small brain?

7. Was T rex a plant eater or a meat eater?

8. Which dinosaur had a long neck and a long tail?

9. How many horns did Triceratops have on its head?

10. Which dinosaur had a powerful club-tail?

11. Which dinosaur had a bony frill on its head?

12. Which dinosaur had bony eyelids?

Answers

1. Stegosaurus.   2. Brachiosaurus was 42 feet (13 meters) or about as tall as three double-decker buses.   3. T rex had short arms.   4. Parasaurolophus.   5. Velociraptor had a sharp claw on the second toe of each foot.   6. Stegosaurus had a small brain.   7. T rex was a meat eater.   8. Brachiosaurus.   9. Triceratops had three horns on its head.   10. Ankylosaurus.   11. Triceratops had a bony frill on its head.   12. Ankylosaurus.

Dictionary

spiky
Something spiky has lots of pointy edges.

armor
Some animals have armor on their body. It can protect them from harm.

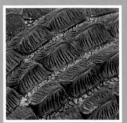

horn
A horn is a piece of bone that grows out of an animal's body. Cows have horns.

attack
If an animal attacks another animal, it is trying to injure or harm it.

crest
A crest grows out of an animal's head.